The History of the Blues

Charles G. Quill

The Rosen Publishing Group's

READING ROOM
Collection

New York

Published in 2003 by The Rosen Publishing Group, Inc.
29 East 21st Street, New York, NY 10010

First Library Edition 2003

Book Design: Michael Flynn

Photo Credits: Cover (King), pp. 1 (King), 19 © Gail Mooney/Corbis; cover (background) © FPG International; pp. 4 (Handy), 10–11, 12 © Bettmann/Corbis; pp. 4 (railroad station), 14–15 (dancing couple), 15 (juke joint) © Corbis; pp. 6–7 (Presley) © SuperStock; pp. 7 (Thornton), 8–9, 15 (Jefferson), 16 (all) © Hulton/Archive; p. 20 © AFP/Corbis; p. 22 © Kevin Fleming/Corbis.

Library of Congress Cataloging-in-Publication Data

Quill, Charles G., 1971-
    The history of the blues / Charles G. Quill.
        p. cm. — (The Rosen Publishing Group's reading room collection)
Includes index.
Summary: Gives a history of blues music from its origins to the present day, with discussions of its African roots and its influence on other music.
    ISBN 0-8239-3706-2 (lib. bdg.)
    1. Blues (Music)—History and criticism—Juvenile literature. [1. Blues (Music)] I. Title. II. Series.
    ML3521 .Q55 1999
    781.643'09—dc21
                                2001007681

Manufactured in the United States of America

For More Information
The World of Music
http://library.thinkquest.org/11315/

The NPR Full List
http://npr.org/programs/specials/vote/dlist.html

Contents

W. C. Handy

No one can say exactly when the blues was invented, but W. C. Handy is one of the people who claimed to have discovered it first.

Birth of the Blues

In 1903, a successful musician and bandleader named W. C. Handy stood on a railroad platform in Mississippi, waiting for the next train home. He could hear thunder in the distance and the hiss of steam from the train, but one sound in particular caught his attention. He later described this unfamiliar, haunting sound as the weirdest music he had ever heard.

What he heard was the blues.

The blues is a type of music that was invented in the southern United States during the late 1800s by African American men and women. Many of these people had been slaves before the **Civil War**. They lived difficult lives. Early blues music often tells stories about their bad luck and trouble. The word "blue" sometimes means "sad."

For many years, blues music was performed mostly by African American musicians. It is now considered one of the most important African American gifts to our **culture**.

The blues is one the most popular kinds of music. It has **influenced** many famous musicians. Almost every style of popular music—country, folk, jazz, rock and roll, rhythm and blues, even rap and hip-hop— is rooted in the blues.

Between 1912 and 1914, W. C. Handy—who had heard that lonely sound in the train station in 1903—wrote and published two songs, "The Memphis Blues" and "The St. Louis Blues." These songs introduced blues music to a bigger audience and helped change American music forever.

6

Elvis Presley

Elvis Presley was one of the most famous rock-and-roll musicians of all time. One of his greatest hits was called "Hound Dog." It was first performed in 1952 by a female blues singer named "Big Mama" Thornton.

Big Mama Thornton

Roots of the Blues

People who study music think the blues began with the folk music of African people who were brought to America hundreds of years ago as slaves. These men, women, and children often sang or **chanted** the music of their native cultures while picking cotton and other crops on southern **plantations**.

The traditional songs slaves sang while working in the fields led to the formation of the blues.

By the late 1700s, this music began to blend with European **religious** musical styles, taking the form of work songs, **field hollers**, and **spirituals**. The blending of these different kinds of music would eventually make a new kind of music called the blues. This is why blues music is considered a truly American musical form.

Early blues music was performed without any musical instruments. Many of these songs were just chants that rhymed. These songs often told stories about people or sad events.

One of the first blues instruments was made from a dried **gourd** with strings attached to it. This instrument eventually became the banjo. The banjo and violin were the main blues instruments used during the 1800s and early 1900s. Later, the guitar replaced the banjo. Today, few blues musicians use banjos, but banjos are still used in other types of music like bluegrass and country.

Other early blues instruments included the jug, the kazoo, the **mandolin**, and the **harmonica**, which was often made to sound like a train whistle. The harmonica is still a popular blues instrument.

Some bands had a person who played the "washtub bass," an instrument made from an upside-down washtub, a broomstick, and a string. It was played by moving the broomstick and plucking the string. ▶

The bottleneck slide was also an important part of the blues sound. Guitarists used the neck from a broken bottle or a piece of pipe and slid it up and down the strings of their guitar or banjo.

N. Carolina

Tennessee

S. Carolina

Arkansas

Georgia

Alabama

Louisiana

Mississippi Delta

Florida

Delta sharecroppers farmed the land in return for farming tools, seeds to plant, and a place to live. These costs were subtracted from the money they made on their crops. ▼

The Mississippi Delta

The **Delta** area in northwestern Mississippi near the Mississippi River had some of the largest plantations in the South in the early 1900s. By this time, the blues had changed from simple work songs into music people could dance to.

In the early 1900s, thousands of African American **sharecroppers** began to move to the Delta area of Mississippi. The Delta's rich soil was good for farming, and the sharecroppers thought they could make money growing crops. Blues musicians followed the sharecroppers to the Delta, hoping they could earn money performing for them.

The Delta became a central meeting place for blues musicians. Once they got to the Delta, they shared ideas and learned a lot from each other. This helped blues music grow and develop.

During the next fifty years, no other area produced more great blues musicians than the Mississippi Delta. Some of the most famous Delta blues musicians included Robert Johnson, Charley Patton, Son House, and Blind Boy Fuller.

Many blues musicians came from other southern states like Alabama, Louisiana, Florida, Georgia, and Texas. They had names like Leadbelly, Blind Lemon Jefferson, Peetie Wheatstraw, and Lightnin' Hopkins. These blues musicians were born in different places throughout the South, but most of them started out playing in the juke joints of the Delta. A juke joint was a place where people could go to eat, drink, listen to music, and dance. The term "juke joint" comes from the word "jukebox." A jukebox is a machine that plays songs when money is put into it.

Blind Lemon Jefferson

Blind Lemon Jefferson was one of the first blues music recording stars. He played in many juke joints before making his first record.

Billie Holiday was a famous singer, but she also wrote many of the songs she sang. ▼

Billie Holiday

Ma Rainey

Bessie Smith

Urban Blues

It was difficult for African American sharecroppers to make money farming. Most of the money they made was spent paying rent for their plot of farmland and their homes, and buying farming supplies. Most sharecroppers were very poor. They wanted better lives for themselves and their families.

From the 1920s through the 1950s, many African American sharecroppers moved north to big cities to get jobs in factories. Again, the blues musicians followed. Before long, cities like Memphis, St. Louis, Kansas City, and Chicago became famous for blues music.

During this time, female blues singers like Bessie Smith and Ma Rainey began to become famous. Billie Holiday, a famous jazz singer, also became known as a great blues singer.

By the late 1940s, blues music had changed with the invention of the electric guitar. Many blues musicians now played in bands that had an electric guitar player, a bass guitar player, and a drummer.

This blues music was much louder than traditional Delta blues music, which made it easier to hear in the bigger cities' noisy music clubs. Muddy Waters, Howlin' Wolf, B. B. King, and John Lee Hooker were among the first musicians to play blues with electric guitars in this new style. Chicago became a huge center for **urban** blues music during this time.

Today, the style of music called "Chicago blues" is really Delta blues played with electric instruments.

One of the most famous of
the urban blues musicians is
B. B. King. "B. B." stands for
"Blues Boy."

19

The Blues Revival

Many African American blues musicians had to struggle to make a living, and some gave up on music entirely. During the 1960s, however, many older blues musicians were "rediscovered" by younger, mostly white audiences. This began a blues **revival**.

The new popularity of these long-forgotten blues musicians introduced their music to thousands of young people who had never heard it before. Many blues musicians had spent years playing on the streets for tips in order to survive. Now they had wider recognition and finally got the respect and money they never had before. This new interest in the blues encouraged younger blues musicians to pursue careers in music.

John Lee Hooker was one of the most successful blues musicians who was "rediscovered" in the 1960s. ◀

The Blues Today

In the years since the blues revival, blues music has become more popular than ever. The blues tradition has been carried on by the older blues musicians who are still alive and by younger artists who grew up listening to these musicians play. Today, nearly every city and town in America has some local blues bands who perform in blues music clubs.

The blues has truly become one of the world's most important and treasured art forms.

Glossary

chant — To call out over and over again.

civil war — A war between two groups of people within a country. The American Civil War was fought between the Northern and Southern states from 1861 to 1865.

culture — The beliefs, customs, art, and religions of a group of people.

Delta — A triangle-shaped area in northwestern Mississippi near the Mississippi River.

field holler — A kind of song that was often sung by slaves while they worked on Southern plantations.

gourd — A fruit that grows on a vine and is related to a pumpkin.

harmonica — A small musical instrument that is played by breathing in and out through different openings.

influence — To affect something.

mandolin — A musical instrument with a pear-shaped body and four to six pairs of metal strings that is played much like a guitar.

plantation — A large cotton, tobacco, or sugarcane farm owned by one family and worked by the people who lived on the land.

religious — Honoring a god or gods.

revival — The act of bringing something old back into use.

sharecropper — A farmer who works another person's land in return for farming supplies and a place to live.

spiritual — An African American religious song.

urban — Having to do with cities or towns.

Index